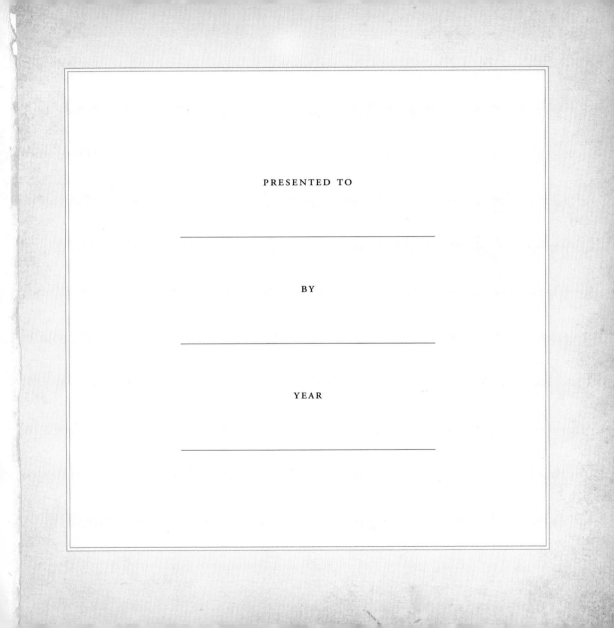

PRESENTED TO

_____

BY

_____

YEAR

_____

Jesus, the Ultimate Gift

Unwrapping the Indescribable Gift of Christmas

LANCE WUBBELS

THOMAS NELSON
Since 1798

NASHVILLE · DALLAS · MEXICO CITY · RIO DE JANEIRO

Jesus, the Ultimate Gift
Copyright © 2011 by Lance Wubbels

Originally published as Jesus Is the Gift, © 2010 by Lance Wubbels.
Published by Inspired Faith, a Simple Truths Company
1952 McDowell Road, Suite 300
Naperville, IL 60563
Toll Free: 888.744.7704
www.inspiredfaith.com

This edition published under license from Inspired Faith exclusively for Thomas Nelson, Inc.

Published in Nashville, Tennessee, by Thomas Nelson. Thomas Nelson is a trademark of Thomas Nelson, Inc.

Designed by Koechel Peterson & Associates, Inc.

Thomas Nelson, Inc., titles may be purchased in bulk for educational, business, fund-raising, or sales promotional use. For information, please e-mail SpecialMarkets@ThomasNelson.com.

All Scripture quotations, unless otherwise indicated, are taken from the HOLY BIBLE: NEW INTERNATIONAL VERSION® (NIV). © 1973, 1978, 1984 by International Bible Society. Used by permission of Zondervan Publishing House. All rights reserved.

Scripture quotations marked NKJV are taken from the NEW KING JAMES VERSION. Copyright © 1982 by Thomas Nelson, Inc. Used by permission. All rights reserved.

The poem "Jesus, the Ultimate Gift" is used by permission of Paula J. Fox, © April 2010.

Photography © Thinkstock.com

ISBN-13: 978-1-4041-9009-2

Printed in China

11 12 13 14 15 RRD 5 4 3 2 1

www.thomasnelson.com

The way to Christmas
     lies through an ancient gate. . . .
a little gate, child-high, child-wide,
and there is a password:

"Peace on earth to men of good will."

May you, this Christmas,
become as a little child again
and enter into His kingdom.

ANGELO PATRI

JESUS CHRIST

true gift

true light

true hope

true joy

CONTENTS

GOD'S ULTIMATE GIFT

He will be great and will be

The angel said to her,

"DO NOT BE AFRAID, MARY,

you have found favor with God.

You will be with child and give birth to a son, and

YOU ARE TO GIVE HIM THE NAME JESUS.

called the Son of the Most High."

LUKE 1:30–32

This past Christmas Eve I took my life into my own hands. I stood in the long entry hallway of a Costco store during the late afternoon as what seemed like hundreds of large empty carts rumbled past me two or three abreast. Frantic last-minute shoppers, mostly men and young people, had fought the good fight for a parking spot and defied me to step into their path and delay their rush to grab a large fluffy robe or a hoodie before time ran out.

In the midst of the busyness of the Christmas season, stampeding with the crowds from one mall store to another, I'm sure you may have wondered the same thing that I was wondering, *Does anyone here even realize what Christmas is about in the first place?*

The apostle John wrote, "For God so loved the world that he gave his one and only Son, that whoever believes in him shall not perish but have eternal life" (John 3:16).

When we consider the meaning of these words, so easily lost in the hustle and bustle of the season, we realize the reason we celebrate Christmas is God's ultimate Gift to man, His Son Jesus Christ.

GOD LOVED.

God gave.

His one and only Son.

As the bells ring out the joys of Christmas, we need to remember that God the Father was the One who began the giving traditions we enjoy today. The world's best Christmas was on the very first Christmas when God gifted mankind with our Savior Jesus Christ. God has, as it were, pulled back the curtain on His glory and love and placed His Son before us. We behold the wonder of the birth of Jesus Christ, the beauty of His life, and the unfathomable grandeur of His person, and we feel overwhelmed that God invites us to come and worship Him.

God became one of us . . . as a baby boy with a tiny smile and two ears and ten fingers and ten toes. Once we see Him for who He really is, we are never the same. ❦

On that first Christmas morning
when Mary kissed her newborn child,
she wasn't just kissing a baby—
she was kissing the face of God.

MARK LOWRY

LATE ON A SLEEPY, STAR-SPANGLED NIGHT,

THOSE ANGELS PEELED BACK THE SKY JUST LIKE YOU WOULD

TEAR OPEN A SPARKLING CHRISTMAS PRESENT.

THEN, WITH LIGHT AND JOY POURING OUT OF HEAVEN

LIKE WATER THROUGH A BROKEN DAM,

THEY BEGAN TO SHOUT AND SING THE MESSAGE THAT BABY

JESUS HAD BEEN BORN. THE WORLD HAD A SAVIOR!

THE ANGELS CALLED IT "GOOD NEWS," AND IT WAS.

LARRY LIBBY

Jesus,
the Ultimate
Gift

He who has not
Christmas in his heart
will never find it under a tree.

ROY L. SMITH

Jesus, God's Indescribable Gift

THANKS BE TO GOD
for his
INDESCRIBABLE
GIFT!

2 CORINTHIANS 9:15

*I*T MIGHT SURPRISE YOU TO LEARN that for a period of time during the Middle Ages, Christmas gift giving was banned by the church due to its suspected pagan origins. It was later justified by the church on the basis that it associated St. Nicholas with Christmas and that the biblical Magi, or wise men, "saw the child with his mother Mary, and they bowed down and worshiped him. Then they opened their treasures and presented him with gifts of gold and of incense and of myrrh" (Matthew 2:11). Giving to others should be a natural expression of our gratitude to the ultimate Gift Giver.

Do you remember the best Christmas gift you ever received? Was it your first doll or favorite stuffed animal or a gold necklace? Perhaps it was your first bike or an XBox 360 or a Sony Playstation or a bucket of Legos. It might have been a storybook or a John Deere tractor.

Mine came around fifty years ago, but I remember it as if it were yesterday. When I was seven years old, over the course of the summer of '59, I made many special bike trips up the dusty gravel road from my boyhood house to our local country store just to take extended gazes at the big box on the highest shelf near the front counter. Well out of a child's reach, that box contained a white safari hunting hat and the most beautiful plastic, big game hunting rifle and scope I'd ever seen. From the first moment I saw it, I ached to have that toy gun in my arms, and I dreamed of the day when I sighted it in on a charging elephant and calmly pulled the trigger.

Then one fateful Saturday morning some time around Halloween, my dreams of safari hunts of tigers and lions suddenly died. I once again rode my bike to the store, and the treasured rifle and hat were gone. The space on the sacred shelf was a cavernous hole, dashing my hopes that somehow, someway that rifle would become mine, even though I knew the gift would be far too expensive for my parents to buy for me. I walked out of the store crushed beyond words, hoping I never ran into the lucky kid who got my gun.

Mercifully, fall gave way to the snow and cold of winter, and the bitterness over the loss of the big game rifle diminished. Eventually Christmas morning arrived, and I jumped out of bed, looking forward to whatever presents had arrived in the night. To my utter shock, among the handful of small presents that sat under the Christmas tree for me, my sister, and my brother was a box so big it hardly fit beneath the tree boughs. It was just too much to even imagine, but that box had my name on it! Ripping off the wrapping, it did indeed contain my heart's desire. That rifle and hat were everything I'd dreamed and more. I have no doubt I was the happiest child in the entire world that blessed morning. 🦌

Let us remember that the Christmas heart is a giving heart,

a wide open heart that thinks of others first.

The birth of the baby Jesus stands

as the most significant event in all history,

because it has meant the pouring into a sick world

the healing medicine of love that has transformed

all manner of hearts for almost two thousand years…

Underneath all the bulging bundles

is this beating Christmas heart.

GEORGE MATTHEW ADAMS

HOW CAN A GIFT BE "INDESCRIBABLE"?

SUDDENLY A GREAT COMPANY

OF THE HEAVENLY HOST APPEARED

WITH THE ANGEL,

PRAISING GOD AND SAYING,

GLORY TO GOD

"*Glory to God in the highest,*

AND ON EARTH PEACE

TO MEN ON WHOM HIS FAVOR RESTS."

LUKE 2:13–14

As wonderful as my best ever Christmas gift was, so wonderful that I can still feel the gun in my hands, let me ask you, "Have you ever received a gift that was beyond description—a gift so good that no words could be found to adequately describe it?" My best gift ever was marvelous, but it surely did not come close to being classified as "indescribable." I can still list off a dozen exacting details regarding that gun.

What kind of gift would it have to be to qualify as being "indescribable," as the apostle Paul states regarding his vision of Jesus Christ? When is a gift so pure *in toto* that it is *beyond recounting, beyond description, beyond being set forth in detail?*

For instance, a gift can be so high tech that we may not even know what it is or what it does, but we can be assured that its manufacturer has described it in such an appealing way as to have enticed someone into believing that it was just the gift we needed.

A gift can be so filled with pleasant memories and emotions that we could never put into words what it means to us, but that in no way limits us from describing the gift itself with precision.

A gift can be so high priced that it staggers our imagination, but that does not make it indescribable. Just ask the marketing team created the ad that tells us we can't live without it.

You see, every man-made gift is describable by someone. And every human gift, even the best ones, including my prized big game hunting rifle, is only temporary. One day, maybe sooner rather than later, our gifts wear out or break, or we outgrow them.

However, the gift of Jesus Christ is not merely "unspeakable" but is beyond words and lasts forever. The greatest gift ever given is the very first gift of Christmas—the person of Jesus. When God gave His one and only Son, He gave the whole world a priceless, indescribable present whose value will not diminish or tarnish over time.

Arnold Toynbee, the great British historian, has said,

And now as we stand indeed with our eyes
fixed upon the further shore,
a single figure rises from the flood
and straightway fills the whole horizon of history.
There stands Jesus, the Savior.

The coming of Jesus Christ is not a mere warm cuddly holiday tradition, but He is Light and Life breaking into human history. His story is our direct link to a loving heavenly Father. The baby born to Mary holds the keys to eternal life. He is full of grace and glory, and we have the opportunity by faith to behold Him who was worthy of the prophets' foretelling, so that we, as the wise men did, might worship our God. ❦

CHRIST IS THE GREAT CENTRAL FACT
OF THE WORLD'S HISTORY.
TO HIM EVERYTHING LOOKS FORWARD OR BACKWARD.
ALL LINES OF HISTORY CONVERGE UPON HIM.
ALL THE GREAT PURPOSES OF GOD
CULMINATE IN HIM.
THE GREATEST AND MOST MOMENTOUS FACT
THAT THE HISTORY OF THE WORLD RECORDS
IS THE FACT OF HIS BIRTH.

CHARLES SPURGEON

Jesus,
the Ultimate
Gift

AN INDESCRIBABLE GIFT BECAUSE OF WHO HE IS

"THE VIRGIN WILL BE WITH CHILD

AND WILL GIVE BIRTH TO A SON,

AND THEY WILL CALL HIM IMMANUEL"

—WHICH MEANS,

"God with us."

MATTHEW 1:23

Three simple words contain the fullness of the Christmas story:

God with us.

Yet who would be so brazen as to claim he or she comprehends the meaning of those words? Who can explain this miracle that transcends all other miracles? How does the infinite, omnipotent, self-existent One, co-equal with God the Father and the Holy Spirit, join Himself with our human nature? How does the uncreated Creator of the heavens and earth become a part of His very own creation?

In Christmas, we celebrate the astonishing, phenomenal generosity and love of God—the marvel and mystery of God loving us so much that He chose to become one of us. Into the midst of the world's problems and pain, the invisible and transcendent God came near in the touchable form of His only Son. The Eternal One stepped into time!

Kevin Vanhoozer has said,

The good news is that
in the face of Jesus Christ
we see the very face of God,
the One who has decided to be with us
and for us in spite of our sin.

Marvelous! Wonderful! *But how?*

No one has ever come close to defining the fullness of what the gift of Jesus Christ means. All of the Church's most thoughtful scholars and theologians have never been able to unfold to us "the mystery of godliness," which the apostle Paul states is "great" (1 Timothy 3:16). How does one possibly put into words what it means for a living man to be able to state, "I and the Father are one" (John 10:30)?

Ignatius of Antioch, an early Church Father, wrote to the church at Ephesus and said this of Jesus:

> VERY FLESH, YET SPIRIT TOO:
> UNCREATED, AND YET BORN;
> GOD AND MAN IN ONE AGREED,
> VERY LIFE-IN-DEATH INDEED.
> FRUIT OF GOD AND MARY'S SEED;
> AT ONCE IMPASSIBLE AND TORN
> BY PAIN AND SUFFERING HERE BELOW;
> JESUS CHRIST, WHOM AS OUR LORD WE KNOW.

How does one understand this?
How do you describe Jesus Christ?

As Charles Spurgeon said, "Jesus Christ was not an angel or a subordinate deity or a being elevated to the Godhead. He was as surely God as God can be, one with the Father and the ever-blessed Holy Spirit. All that God means, the infinite Jehovah with us, this was worthy of the burst of the midnight song when angels startled the shepherds with their carols. . . . *God*—therein is the glory; *God with us*—therein is the grace. Let us admire this truth. Let us stand at a reverent distance from it as Moses when he saw God in the bush and put off his shoes, feeling that the place where he stood was holy ground. This is a wonderful fact: *God the infinite dwelt in the frail body of a lowly man.*"

The Son is the
RADIANCE OF GOD'S GLORY
and the exact representation
of his being,
sustaining all things
BY HIS POWERFUL WORD.

HEBREWS 1:3

We are quickly lost in mysteries when we attempt to comprehend the person of Jesus Christ.

He is not merely a good man or even a superman; He is God in human flesh.

He is not half God and half man.

He is not merely a man who "had God within Him" or a man who "manifested the God principle."

We come face to face with One who is fully divine and fully man. The divine One has condescendingly taken upon Himself our humanity, and He is most truly man. The divine nature was not changed or altered. He is God, the second person of the Trinity.

*For in Christ
all the fullness
of the Deity
lives in
bodily form.*

COLOSSIANS 2:9

Yet while these are accurate theological descriptions, none of our interpretations fathoms their depth or begins to explain the absolutely infinite, uncreated God coming to us as one of us. He was truly the person of God clothed as a baby and lying in a lowly manger, then later walking freely among us that He might untie all of the knots and tangles in our confused and twisted ideas about God and ourselves and about life. He was God wrapped up in human form, coming close that we might be given the unbelievable opportunity to know Him— not exhaustively, but to truly know Him.

It boggles the mind to think that the King of kings and Lord of lords was born to a young virgin peasant girl in Bethlehem! We are left to shake our heads in wonder and say with those who watched Him perform His miracles, "What manner of Man is this?" We are given a glimpse into the divine nature, and He shines with all the fullness of divine glory we would ever expect.

But we can never plunge to discern His depths or soar to His heights or journey to His limitless horizon. Our finite thoughts can no more capture the Savior God than a child can capture the ocean by bottling up a little saltwater in a plastic bottle at the beach.

Jesus is truly indescribable. We stand and gaze upon His boundless person and are left to a lifetime of contemplation . . . and to worship before the One who was with God and who was God. Is there any doubt that throughout eternity we will forever speak with wonder about the miracle and the mystery of His coming?

Stepping from the throne,

HE REMOVED HIS ROBE OF LIGHT

and wrapped himself in skin:

pigmented, human skin.

THE LIGHT OF THE UNIVERSE

ENTERED A DARK, WET WOMB.

He whom angels worship nestled himself in the placenta of a peasant, was birthed into the cold night, and then slept on cow's hay. MAX LUCADO

JESUS CHRIST *was born into this world,*
not from it.
He did not emerge out of history;
He came into history from the outside.

JESUS CHRIST *is not the best human being*
the human race can boast of—
HE IS A BEING *for whom the human race*
can take no credit at all.
HE IS NOT MAN *becoming God,*
but God Incarnate—
GOD COMING INTO HUMAN FLESH *from outside it.*

His life is the highest
and the holiest entering through
the most humble of doors.

OSWALD CHAMBERS

Jesus, the Ultimate Gift

An indescribable Gift
because of what He came to do

She [Mary] will give birth to a son,
and you are to give him the name Jesus,
because he will save his people
from their sins.

MATTHEW 1:21

Handel H. Brown has noted,

The shepherds did not go to Bethlehem

seeking the birth of a great man,

or a famous teacher, or a national hero.

THEY WERE PROMISED A SAVIOR.

Although nothing is wrong with most of the glitter and glamour of the Christmas season, it does tend to obscure the real meaning of the celebration of God's Gift to the world. When the shepherds went to Bethlehem to see this Gift, they found a newborn boy in a manger, the most lowly of places. Nevertheless, they didn't look farther for a baby prince who looked more royal. They accepted God's free Gift as our Savior.

Jesus stated that His purpose in coming was "to seek and to save the lost." We had built up personal mountains of sin and offenses against God, and there was nothing we could do on our own to change it. Jesus came so that we could be brought into a relationship with God. Without Jesus' perfect sacrifice on the cross for us, we would have been without hope and separated from God forever. The death and endless suffering due to us because of our sins was paid by His infinite sacrifice. Only the Son of God could become the Lamb that was slain for the sins of humankind. Jesus is the ultimate Gift because of His purpose in coming to earth.

John saw Jesus coming toward him,

and said, "Behold! The Lamb of God

who takes away the sin of the world!"

. . . the Lamb slain from the foundation of the world.

JOHN 1:29; REVELATION 13:8 NKJV

The cross always stands near the manger.

AMY CARMICHAEL

Salvation started with the birth of the Christ Child in a manger in Bethlehem, but it ended with the death of the man Jesus Christ on a cross just outside of Jerusalem. Salvation started with angels singing "glory to God in the highest," but it ended when a Roman centurion and those who were guarding Jesus exclaimed "surely he was the Son of God!" Salvation started with promise in the Garden of Eden that the offspring of the woman would "crush" the serpent's head, but the serpent would strike his heel. Salvation ended with Isaiah telling us that "he was pierced for our transgressions, he was crushed for our iniquities; the punishment that brought us peace was upon him, and by his wounds we are healed."

Can anyone describe what it cost God the Father to send His Son to save us? Can you begin to even remotely imagine how much God loved us to send His one and only Son to earth, knowing it would cost Jesus His life so we could have eternal life? Who can tell what the Father felt when His dear Son entered a world that was determined to kill Him . . . from His birth? To be despised, spit upon, mistreated, hung up like a thief, and made to bear infinite agony for our sin—what was that like for the Father?

Or can you imagine how much Jesus loved us to be willing to come and ultimately die on the cross so that we could have access to eternal life? Indescribable were Christ's sufferings when He was made sin for us . . . when He cried out, "My God, my God, why have you forsaken me?" God placed all of our sins on the shoulders of His Son. Jesus drank the full cup of divine punishment that should have been ours—He paid it all. God agreed that all of our sins would be forgiven by the death of that one perfect man if we would only put our faith in Him and agree to make Him the Lord of our lives.

Who can declare the greatness of His sacrifice? Think of the glory of the eternal Christ at the Father's right hand, and remember that all this was laid aside in His descent to becoming a man. Consider His infinite perfections and the shameful contempt that was poured out upon Him. Every step of His way was full of love and wonders. We have seen that His becoming one with us as a man is a miracle beyond our reasoning, but even more so is His substitution, His taking our place.

"He breathed our air,
felt our pain,
knew our sorrows,
and died for our sins."

CHARLES SWINDOLL

Even if we could speak with the tongues of men and of angels, we would never come close to describing the fullness of the great redemption, the matchless death of Jesus Christ for us. His wondrous condescending love in taking our place, His standing in our place that we might stand in His place and be accepted in the Beloved—this carries our heart away. The Gift is indescribable when we have spoken and written our very best, and so let this suffice: Our hearts swell with gratitude; our eyes overflow.

Gaze into the great abyss of God's heart. Be sure of this, that the depth of His love is unfathomable. It is futile to attempt a definition of infinity, and therefore vain to hope to declare how wide, how high, how deep, how broad is the wondrous Gift of God to us. Thank God our inability to comprehend it did not keep Him from coming.

Max Lucado once asked the poignant question:

Upon learning that God would rather die than live without you,
how do you react?
How can you begin to explain such passion?

HAVE YOU ANSWERED
THAT QUESTION?

GOD'S PLAN OF SALVATION has existed since time began.

Only He—in His wisdom, love, power, and perfection—

could have devised such a deeply compelling

yet incredibly costly plan.

ONLY A GOD as infinitely loving as our God

would be willing to let His sinless Son serve

as the perfect and acceptable sacrifice

for the sin of the human race.

HENRY & RICHARD BLACKABY

The Christmas message is that there is hope
for a ruined humanity—
    hope of pardon,
    hope of peace with God,
    hope of glory—
because at the Father's will Jesus became poor,

and was born in a stable

so that thirty years later

HE MIGHT HANG ON A CROSS.

J. I. PACKER

AN INDESCRIBABLE
GIFT BECAUSE
OF HIS GRACE

Through the tender mercy of our God,

with which the Dayspring

from on high has visited us;

to give light to those who sit in darkness

and the shadow of death,

to guide our feet into the way of peace.

LUKE 1:78–79 NKJV

Truth to tell, typically the gifts we give at Christmas are given because the recipients of those gifts have some relationship to us. We buy a gift for our spouse and children because they are our intimate family. We may buy gifts for other family members because they are family. If we buy a gift for someone who is not family, it is probably because they gave us a gift last year and we feel obligated. On the other hand, we don't give gifts to the person who has been slandering our name or to the angry neighbor who never has a kind word to say.

Jesus is the ultimate Gift because of the grace by which He was given. This is what makes His Gift so special. He doesn't owe us a thing. We were in constant rebellion against Him and His will for our lives. With that in mind, the apostle Paul says something remarkable, "But God demonstrates his own love for us in this: While we were still sinners, Christ died for us" (Romans 5:8).

Love came down at Christmas;
Love all lovely, love divine;
Love was born at Christmas,
Star and angels gave the sign.

CHRISTINA GEORGINA ROSSETTI

God gives His Gift, not because He feels obligated to give a gift, but because His love is so overwhelming. Grace is not only God's undeserved favor, but it is favor shown to the one who has deserved the very opposite. It is a pure gift of grace, a gift beyond our ability ever to comprehend. The Gift of God's love in Jesus is ours. It is ours whether we are aware of the Christ Child or not. He is a perfect Gift of grace, whether we believe it or not. And there are no words adequate to describe God's grace toward us in Jesus.

Christmas is all about "the tender mercy of our God, With which the Dayspring from on high has visited us; To give light to those who sit in darkness and the shadow of death, to guide our feet into the way of peace" (Luke 1:78–79 NKJV). The birth of Jesus was like a majestic sunrise after a night of darkness. Christ was the Dayspring who had come in the fullness of time to dispel the darkness and usher in the kingdom of God. Jesus is "the light of the world" (John 8:12), providing the way of salvation to men and women sitting in such a desperate condition—separated from God.

This is Christmas—

THE REAL MEANING OF IT.

God loving, searching, giving Himself—

TO US.

Man's needing, receiving, giving himself—

TO GOD.

This is the meaning of Christmas—

THE WONDER AND GLORY OF IT.

RUTH BELL GRAHAM

What confidence this should inspire in our hearts! The fullness from which we derive the grace we receive is none other than the infinite fullness of God! And throughout His lifetime on earth, Jesus rendered entire and undeviating obedience to the law of God, having taken upon Himself the form of a servant. In always doing His Father's will, through His suffering, death, resurrection, and ascension, Jesus finished the redemptive work that His Father gave Him to do. Now there is "a fountain filled with blood drawn from Immanuel's veins" whose fullness can never be exhausted by all the sin of man. In Jesus there is an infinity of grace and truth.

Neither the Old Testament prophecies nor the chronicles of time could ever contain the highest manifestation of the glory of God—the all-conquering love that took Jesus to the death of the cross. His words were wise; His touch was healing; His character was flawless beauty; His miracles, amazing. But the very heart of Christ's gift to us is the gift of His very life to be the life of our lives. In the cross, Jesus Christ revealed the fullness of God's heart—infinite in love and grace—the very being of God.

And so it is that grace comes to you and me like waves of the sea—one grace has hardly come into our soul when there follows another. God gives grace in preparation for further grace—the grace for a broken heart; the grace to turn away from sin and place our faith in Jesus; the grace to truly know Jesus and be changed into His image.

Are you willing to believe

THAT GOD'S GRACE

IS STRONGER THAN SIN

or hate or bitterness

or the powers of darkness

or death itself?

grace

If the streams of grace are fathomless,

who shall measure the source?

If grace is as high and as boundless as heaven,

is not divine love an unutterable mercy?

Who can describe heavenly things?

How can earth describe Him?

THE HEART OF CHRIST
BECAME LIKE A RESERVOIR
IN THE MIDST OF THE MOUNTAINS.
ALL THE TRIBUTARY STREAMS OF INIQUITY,
AND EVERY DROP OF THE SINS
OF HIS PEOPLE, RAN DOWN AND GATHERED
INTO ONE VAST LAKE, DEEP AS HELL AND
SHORELESS AS ETERNITY.
ALL THESE MET, AS IT WERE,
IN CHRIST'S HEART,
AND HE ENDURED THEM ALL.

CHARLES SPURGEON

THE EXTENT OF GOD'S LOVE AT CALVARY
IS SEEN IN BOTH THE INFINITE COST TO HIM
OF GIVING HIS ONE AND ONLY SON,
AND IN THE WRETCHED AND MISERABLE
CONDITION OF THOSE HE LOVED.

God could not remove our sins without an

infinite cost to both Himself and His Son.

And because of their great love for us, both were willing—yes, more than merely willing—to pay that great cost, the Father in giving His one and only Son, and the Son in laying down His life for us. One of the essential characteristics of love is the element of self-sacrifice, and this was demonstrated for us to its ultimate in God's love at Calvary. | JERRY BRIDGES

An indescribable gift because of His effect on us

Just as the Son of Man
did not come to be served,

BUT TO SERVE,

and to give his life

as a ransom for many.

MATTHEW 20:28

WHEN WE OPEN OUR GIFTS AT CHRISTMAS, we might be thrilled . . . or mildly pleased . . . or even, on occasion, disappointed, but at the end of the day, we're the same person we were before the gifts. Such is not the case when we receive God's Gift. The Bible teaches that when we accept Jesus, we will never be the same again, because of how He affects our lives.

THE FIRST EFFECT OF JESUS COMING INTO OUR LIVES IS THAT WE ARE FORGIVEN. Because Jesus is now our Savior, our sins are forgiven. God has forgotten them; He will not remember them, and He buries them as deep as the sea. We don't have to live in guilt anymore, because God takes the guilt away when we accept His free gift of Jesus. We are washed in His blood, clothed in the righteousness of the Son of God.

Have you experienced the joy of knowing that all your sins are gone? Your sins are paid for, and your eternal life with God is purchased. "For the wages of sin is death, but the gift of God is eternal life in Christ Jesus our Lord" (Romans 6:23). You have the receipt in your hand, written in the very blood of the One who paid the price. Christ's record of that payment is forever settled in His book, the Bible!

SECOND, WHEN WE ACCEPT THE GIFT OF JESUS, WE ARE ADOPTED INTO HIS FAMILY AND GIVEN CITIZENSHIP IN HIS KINGDOM. Before, we were strangers and aliens, separated from God. But now, because we have accepted Him, we are adopted as sons and daughters of the Almighty God. In New Testament language, the word used by God for *adoption* means "placed into a family as an adult son." This denotes our standing in God's family: we enter God's family not as little children but as adult sons with all the privileges. Everything that belongs to Jesus also belongs to us. We are adopted into the family of the Eternal, made to be brothers and sisters and joint heirs with Christ in God's family, because we have accepted His indescribable Gift.

THIRD, WHEN WE ACCEPT JESUS, WE RECEIVE THE GIFT OF HIS HOLY SPIRIT TO LIVE WITHIN US. Because of our sin, we were dead in our trespasses and sin. Our only hope of getting into God's family is by regeneration or "the new birth" through the Holy Spirit (John 3:3). Christ died to fill us with endless life and to make us brand new—that's regeneration! "And you He made alive, who were dead in trespasses and sins" (Ephesians 2:1 NKJV).

Have you experienced the power of a redeemed life and what it's like to daily partake of the powerful presence of the very Lord God Almighty? Now He will guide and counsel and protect and empower us. We are never alone, because He is always with us.

AND FOURTH, WE ARE GIVEN GOD'S PEACE. Because of our sin, we were enemies of God; so we need reconciliation. Christ died to take enemies and make them friends—that's reconciliation! A sinner stands before God as an enemy and is made a friend by Christ's peace. "Therefore, having been justified by faith, we have peace with God through our Lord Jesus Christ" (Romans 5:1 NKJV). Not the peace of the world, but the peace that passes all understanding. Peace that allows us to cope with everyday situations.

we have peace through Christ

Jesus is the ultimate Gift ever given

because of His effect on us!

It will take an eternity for us to comprehend the effects of the Gift of Jesus in our lives, let alone to try to describe their fullness. Even in this lifetime, if we have Christ in our lives, what is there that we do not have? If we lose everything but Christ, what have we lost? Every other person, possession, and gift can be stripped away from us by death, sickness, disaster, or some other means. Only Jesus will never leave us or be lost; only He can save and keep us forever. Why should we fret over this or that when God has given us His Son?

The infinite God has provided an infinite salvation, infinite love, and infinite mercy. It's an everlasting covenant ordered in all things, of which the substance and the seal is an infinite Christ. Christ is the indescribable Gift of God.

This is Christmas:

not the tinsel,

not the giving and receiving,

not even the carols,

BUT THE HUMBLE HEART THAT RECEIVES ANEW

THE WONDROUS GIFT, THE CHRIST.

FRANK MCKIBBEN

Who can add to Christmas?

The perfect motive is that God so loved the world.

The perfect gift is that He gave His only Son.

The only requirement is to believe in Him.

The reward of faith is that you shall have everlasting life.

CORRIE TEN BOOM

Unwrapping the Indescribable Gift of Jesus

Yet to all who received him,
to those who believed in his name,
*   he gave the right to become*
*   children of God . . .*

JOHN 1:12

MAX LUCADO OBSERVED, "God's gifts shed light on God's heart, God's good and generous heart. His gifts came, not wrapped in paper, but in passion. Not placed around a tree but a cross. And not covered with ribbons, but sprinkled with blood. The gifts of the cross."

Just like any other gift, we can't enjoy the benefits of the Gift of Jesus unless we first receive it. Do you hear the passion in God's voice as He offers you the "the good news" of the gospel and says, "Come to me . . . and I will give you rest"? Do you see His Cross and the passion of the divine Lover of your life? What better time than right now to believe the Good News of great joy that the angels sang about, to accept what God has done on our behalf.

My prayer is that you will know that God's priceless gift is for you! And that you too will open your heart to receive Jesus and fall at His feet and worship Him.

God has given us the most valuable Gift possible: His one and only Son on our behalf so that we can be restored to a relationship with Him. To receive the free gift of Jesus is not difficult. All we need to do is first recognize our sins and ask God to forgive us of those sins. Second, we need to believe that Jesus paid our punishment for those sins—that there was nothing we could do to pay for our sins. And finally, we need to commit to living His way versus our way.

And if we have received Jesus in the past, let's not neglect this relationship that God has so dearly bought at the cost of Jesus' own life. You might want to think about whether you've been, in a sense, keeping that Gift on display. Amid the cares of everyday living, it can be easy to let God's Gift get pushed aside. Christmas offers a perfect time to ask ourselves: Are we growing? Are we following through? If not, then we're not enjoying the full power God wants us to have in this life.

YOU CAN NEVER TRULY ENJOY CHRISTMAS
until you can look up into the Father's face
and tell him you have received
His Christmas Gift.

JOHN R. RICE

To believe on Christ, I say:

not merely to believe in Him,

or to believe something about Him,

but to believe on Him;

and this means to

ENTRUST YOUR SOUL TO HIM

and to trust in Him for wisdom
and strength and salvation.

WASHINGTON GLADDEN

Jesus, the

Ultimate Gift

by Paula J. Fox

God sent a very special Gift
that's personally for you.
An incomparable expression of His love,
and here's a clue . . .

It's everything you've wished for,
even better than you thought.
And it won't cost you a penny;
In fact, it can't be bought.

Designed to be a perfect fit
for hearts of every size,
    This Gift will change your life
    and it will open up your eyes.

It will give your life more beauty;
you'll discover why you're here.
    You'll see with greater vision
    as His purpose becomes clear.

Sometimes a gift has strings attached,
which surely isn't fair.
    But this one offers freedom
    from each burden that you bear.

It's the best deal of a lifetime,
and it has a guarantee.
    It will be with you forever
    and throughout eternity.

Now you're probably imagining
just what this Gift might be,
    And perhaps you're thinking,
    How could it be quite so wonderful for me?

A Gift beyond what human
understanding can conceive,
    It's more than you would dare to think,
    imagine, or believe.

You won't find another like it
any place upon this earth—
　　Jesus is the ultimate Gift,
　　One of a kind right from His birth.

He's called *Immanuel,*
which means that "God will be with you."
　　He's the Gift that keeps on giving,
　　always faithful through and through.

Superior in every way;
none other can compare.
　　He is greater and more powerful
　　than you'll find anywhere.

But there is one more bonus
with this Gift, as you shall see:
　　　　A home for you in paradise,
　　　　and He's the master key.

Oh, how could you refuse this Gift
that opens heaven's doors,
　　　　Especially when it comes from God . . .

signed *"Personally yours."*

Thanks be to God

FOR HIS

INDESCRIBABLE GIFT.

2 CORINTHIANS 9:15

His life is matchless,

and His goodness is limitless.

His mercy is enough,

and His grace is sufficient.

His reign is righteous,

His yoke is easy,

and His burden is light.

He is indestructible.

He is indescribable.

He is incomprehensible.

He is inescapable.

He is invincible.

He is irresistible.

He is irrefutable.

My Jesus is . . .

EVERYTHING.

ANNE GRAHAM LOTZ

LANCE WUBBELS is the vice president of literary development at Koechel Peterson & Associates, Inc., a Minneapolis-based design and publishing firm, and Bronze Bow Publishing. Before joining Koechel Peterson, he worked as the managing editor of Bethany House Publishers for eighteen years and taught biblical courses at Bethany College of Missions in Bloomington, Minnesota.

Wubbels has authored several fiction and nonfiction books, including *If Only I Knew, Dance While You Can,* and *I Wish for You,* which are bestselling gift books with Hallmark. He has published two gift books with Inspired Faith, *A Time for Prayer* and *To a Child Love Is Spelled T-I-M-E,* which won a 2005 Gold Medallion award from the Evangelical Christian Publishers Association. His novel, *One Small Miracle,* won an Angel Award, and his 365-day devotional, *In His Presence,* also won a Gold Medallion award.

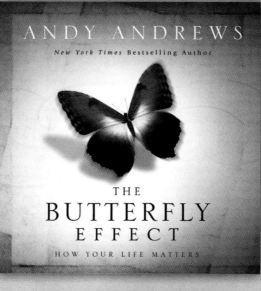

ANDY ANDREWS

New York Times Bestselling Author

THE
BUTTERFLY
EFFECT

HOW YOUR LIFE MATTERS

ISBN: 978-1-4041-8780-1 e-Book: 978-0-5291-2429-6

HOW THE DECISIONS YOU MAKE TODAY HAVE MORE IMPACT THAN YOU REALIZE.

Speaker and *New York Times* bestselling author Andy Andrews shares a compelling and powerful story about a decision one man made more than a hundred years ago and the ripple effect it's had on us individually, and nationwide, today. It's a story that will not only inspire courage and wisdom in our decisions but also affect the way we treat others through our lifetime.

AVAILABLE AT BOOKSTORES EVERYWHERE.